GW00597327

THIS BOOK
BELONGS TO

4

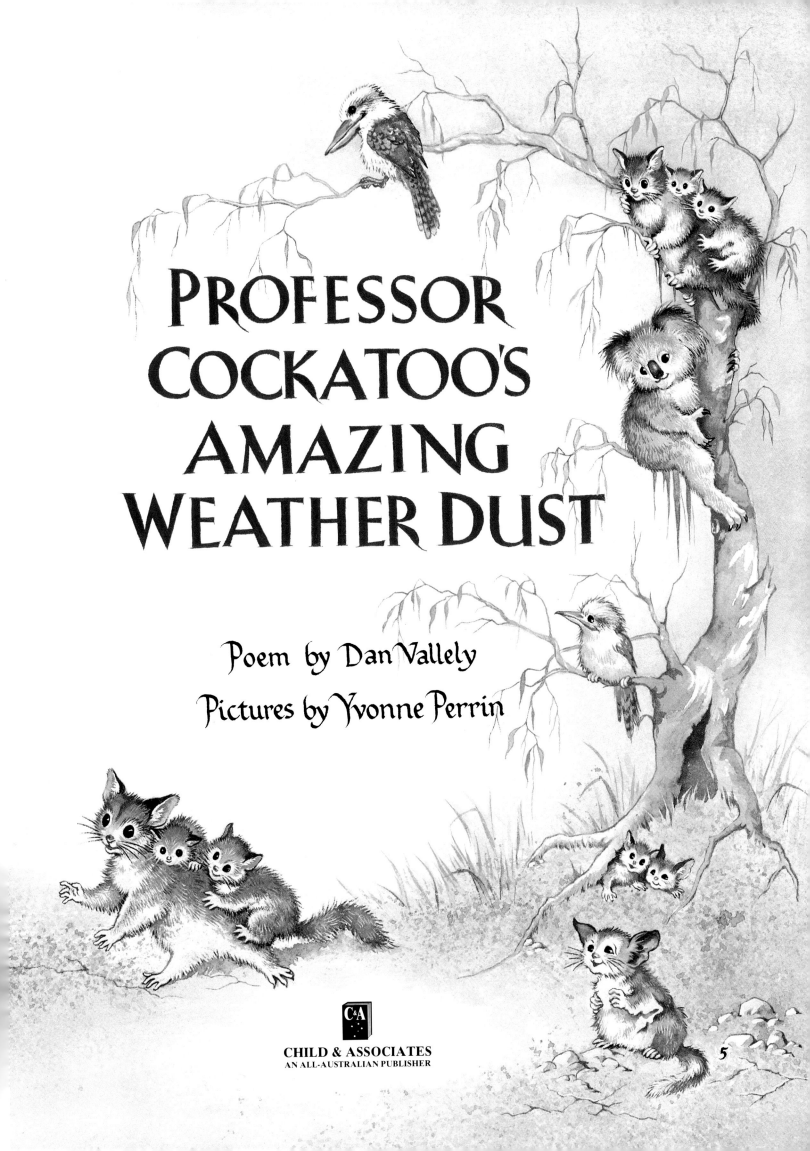

PROFESSOR COCKATOO'S AMAZING WEATHER DUST

Poem by Dan Vallely

Pictures by Yvonne Perrin

CHILD & ASSOCIATES
AN ALL-AUSTRALIAN PUBLISHER

5

6

It was spring in Possum Creek
But the future seemed quite bleak,
For a cruel drought held sway upon the land.
The lake was drying fast
And they knew it wouldn't last.
In short a dreadful crisis was at hand.

7

Tom Echidna trusty Mayor,
With rare judgement did declare,
"There is one whose brilliant mind may hold the clue,
To save us from disaster,
Send for Possum Creek's headmaster,
That gifted bird, Professor Cockatoo."

Unknown to friends and neighbours,
That wise scholar in his labours
On that problem had been working day and night.
And had, as it transpired,
In the end though greatly tired,
Made a substance which might save them from their plight.

9

The following day at noon
Aboard a great balloon
Stepped the gallant band who'd vowed to save the day.
Whilst the good Professor fussed,
Checking bags of weather dust,
They untied the rope and slowly sailed away.

11

12

Big Red Kangaroo, as planned,
Took charge of ballast sand.
Ed Galah stood by a cannon of great size.
Wally Wombat steered the craft
And Peter Possum stationed aft,
With Platypus, kept watch with anxious eyes.

13

They fired a practice round
To ensure the gun was sound,
But, alas, the Flying Doctor was close by.
With his aircraft blown to shreds,
He wrecked several chicken sheds
And crash-landed in Tim Wallaby's pigsty.

14

The crew, quite sad of face,
Filled the gun with half a case
Of weather dust and lit the fuse with care.
A mighty boom resounded
And the creatures stood dumbfounded
As a mass of swirling snowflakes filled the air.

16

The blizzard still increasing
Showed little sign of ceasing.
Icy breezes lashed the bushland folk.
Where the sun had just been blazing
They gaped at scenes amazing
As the bush lay white beneath a wintry cloak.

LAKE WONGI

17

Another boom much louder
Indicated extra powder
Had been used to try to rectify the mess.
The blizzard, changing form,
Became a wild electric storm
But as for rain, they'd still had no success.

This time, the gun, reloaded
With a mite too much, exploded
Scattering the crew both far and wide.
Cockatoo and Ed Galah
Were the luckiest by far
And flew away with little hurt but pride.

21

Platypus with graceful arc
Came down inside the park
Upon a hornet's nest, as fate decreed.
The occupants of course
Protested with such force
That he departed shortly after at great speed.

Peter Possum somersaulted
Until his progress halted
At the dairy in a tub of cottage cheese.
Wally Wombat, always brave,
Caused a mini-tidal wave
As he hit Lake Wongi, backwards if you please.

COTTAGE
CHEESE

LAKE WONGI

24

Big Red, reluctant flyer,
Struck the Town Hall spire
And quickly tumbled off towards the ground,
To land with doubtful luck
Upon the garbage truck
Which was passing at the moment on its round.

Their tribulations ended
With the heroes well attended
In the hospital, a sick and sorry lot.
But wondrous pouring rain
Soon washed away their pain
And exhausted, each slept soundly in his cot.

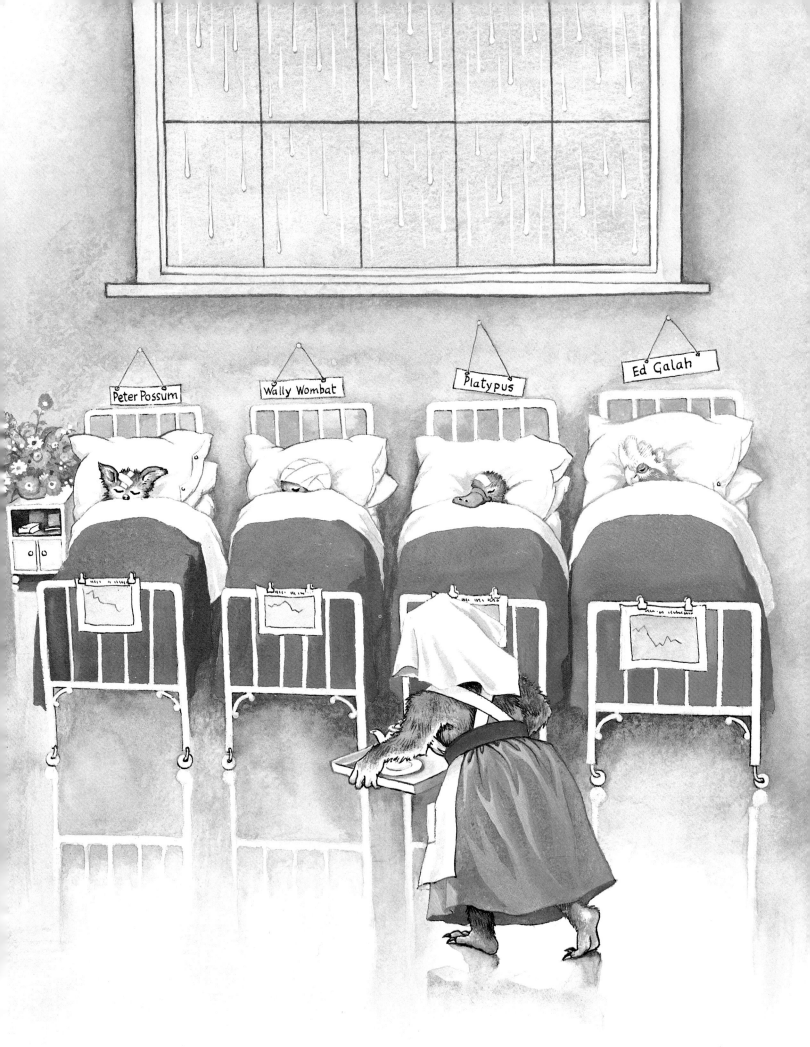

Thus the gallant few,
With their share of luck it's true,
Put an end to Possum Creek's worst ever drought,
With good old Aussie grit,
They stood the test and mastered it.
We shall hear from them again, I have no doubt.

Published by
Child & Associates Publishing Pty Ltd
5 Skyline Place, Frenchs Forest, NSW, Australia, 2086

First edition 1983
Reprinted 1986
Reprinted 1988
Paperback edition April 1989
Reprinted September 1989
Poem © Dan Vallely 1983, 1989
Illustrations © Yvonne Perrin 1983, 1989
Printed in Hong Kong by Everbest Printing Co. Ltd
National Library of Australia Card Number and
ISBN 0 86777 031 7